IFWG Publishing Chapbooks

Black Moon (Eugen Bacon) 2020
Tool Tales (Kaaron Warren & Ellen Datlow) 2021
Stark Naked (Silvia Cantón Rondoni) 2021
Infectious Hope (Silvia Cantón Rondoni, ed.) 2021

An IFWG Publishing Chapbook

Infectious Hope

poems of hope & resilience from the pandemic

edited by Silvia Cantón Rondoni

Printed in Palatino Linotype and FreightNeo Pro.

IFWG Publishing International

www.ifwgpublishing.com

IFWG
Publishing

Table of Contents

Foreword by Lee Murray...1

Preface To Infectious Hope by the editor................................5

Linda D. Addison... HERE/NOW...6

Ryka Aoki... HUNGRY ONCE AGAIN, IN AMERICA.....................8

Crisosto Apache... A PRAYER FOR US—*Ik ł'dá beedaajindánde*.............10

Allen Ashley... SYMPTOMS MAY VARY....................................12

Eugen Bacon... WHAT THE MASK SAW.....................................14

Esther Belin... WASHING DISHES IS GOOD MEDICINE...................16

Jenny Blackford... THE DANCE...18

Isobelle Carmody... THE CHICKENS OF THE APOCALYPSE...........20

Jay Caselberg... CHRYSALIS..22

Anne Casey... WHERE GULLS CRY...24

Kat Clay... SMALL CHOICES..26

Claire G. Coleman... I CANNOT SING WITH THE RIVER.................28

PS Cottier... PATTERNS...30

Cardinal Cox... BEFORE THE DAWN...32

Jack Dann... HOUSE ARREST...34

Sebastien Doubinsky... IS POETRY CONTAGIOUS?......................36

Nigel Ellis... IN THE TIME OF BREATHING................................38

Stephanie Ellis... ANOTHER EVE...40

Rebecca Fraser... #breathe...42

Owl Goingback... QUIET STARS..44

Oz Hardwick... THE TROCADERO SHOPPING MALL....................46

Dominique Hecq... FIVE DAYS IN FOUR HUNDRED WORDS...........48

Dominic Hoey... THEY ONLY BECOME DREAMS
WHEN YOU WAKE..50

Robert Hood... THE BALLAD OF THE MONSTERS 2020....................52

Roz Kaveney... PERSIST...54

Joe R. Lansdale... THE MOMENT PASSES..................................56

Steph Lum... RECREATE..58

Alessandro Manzetti... WHEN SHE LEFT.................................60

Kirstyn Mcdermott... UNTOUCHED.......................................62

Donna McLeod... *Ka whawhai tonu mātou*.............................64

Fiona Murphy... PERPETUAL STASIS....................................66

Jason Nahrung... GROUNDED..68

Biola Olatunde... THE UNBUCKLING.....................................70

Yenn Purkis... A HAPPY THOUGHT.......................................72

Dan Rabarts... DISJOINTED..74

Hester J. Rook... the things that would not have happened,
were it not for this...76

Sumiko Saulson... WITH DECEMBER COMES ELUNE.........................78

Angela Yuriko Smith... A NEW MATCH..................................80

Ruby Smith... HOME ALONE...82

Christina Sng... OUR BRIEF TIME IN THE SUN..........................84

Heather Truett... GHAZAL FOR THE GOOD IN 2020.......................86

Kyla Lee Ward... WARDROBE MALFUNCTION...............................88

Janeen Webb... HOTEL QUARANTINA.....................................90

Adam Wolfond... IN THE HEART OF MUSIC OPENS HOPE............92

Tabatha Wood... OF TIME AND TIDE....................................94

Fiona Wright... *& normal*..96

Marty Young... AN ENDLESS BARRAGE...................................98

Foreword

As I write this foreword to *Infectious Hope*, the global COVID pandemic is still raging, its fallout immeasurable. Precious loved ones have been lost, economies stripped, inequalities laid bare. Yet, this isn't the apocalypse we'd expected. Far easier to face a horde of staggering zombies or a constellation of alien spaceships a-hover on the horizon. At least then we might actually *do* something. Fire off a few missiles. Barricade the street. Instead, our current enemy is invisible, insidious, and frighteningly indefinite. Our best recourse is to sequester ourselves from all human connection, to sit on the couch in our pyjamas, and wait for salvation. Now a year on from those first terrifying days, our forbearance is wearing thin. We've read books, binge-watched shows, and baked banana bread. By now, our nerves are frazzled, our relationships strained. Funds are low. Friends and family members are missing in action. How will we go on? How will we survive? And what will the world look like if we do?

I'm delighted to attest that in *Infectious Hope*, forty-seven of the world's best poets respond to these questions with verve and insight. *Infectious Hope* is a startling work—'lit from within with an otherworldly luminosity' to borrow Anne Casey's image in *Where Gulls Cry*—and an important one. Covering a range of styles, structures, and intensities, and representing diverse voices from across the globe, the poems in this work are personal, poignant, and undeniably potent. The poems' titles tell a story in themselves: consider Jason Nahrung's *Grounded*, Jack Dann's *House Arrest*, Fiona Murphy's *Perpetual Stasis*, Janeen Webb's *Hotel Quarantina*, Stephanie Ellis's *Another Eve*, and Dan Rabarts's *Disjointed*, all works highlighting our instant isolation and growing disconnectedness.

Many of the poems reflect on the relentlessness nature of our new quotidian, conjured, for example, in 'a single blue heron' (*Ghazal for the Good in 2020*, Heather Truett), 'a picture of a coffee cup on a Zoom call' (*Recreate*, Steph Lum), 'cornflakes at the bottom of the box' (*Home Alone*, Ruby Smith), a Persian rug in the dining room (*When She Left*, Alessandro Manzetti), and terms like 'SunMonTuesWed-Bleughday' (*Symptoms May Vary*, Allen Ashley) which were unprecedented before this strange new-normal.

Masks are front and centre in Joe R. Lansdale's comic-horror poem, *The Moment Passes*. 'I think I must mask in the shower' he writes. In Lansdale's pandemic, even the roaches wear masks.

Supermarket shelves, hand sanitiser, and sinks full of dishes also feature heavily. Breath and breathing, and #breathe, are mentioned more than once. We are 'becalmed with each new breath' writes Tabbatha Wood in *Of Time and Tide*.

Some of the poems, like Owl Goingback's *Quiet Stars*, a tribute to his mother, ache with the pain and tenderness of loss. Other poems brim with hope, like Sumiko Saulson's *With December Comes Elune*, which sings with renewed promise at the safe arrival of a treasured child. Poet Crisosto Apache also offers hope, envisaging our future with *A Prayer for Us–Ikłdá beedaajindánde*, Yenn Purkis dreams *A Happy Thought* into being while dancing in front of a bedroom mirror, and Jay Caselberg speaks of emerging from our cocoons to gleaming new possibilities in *Chrysalis*. In the 'imagined fragile spaces' of our new existence, Grandmaster Linda D. Addison reflects on the fecklessness of time, her poem, *Here/Now*, reminding us to live in the moment and to appreciate each day, each breath, a sentiment echoed by Christina Sng in the exquisite *Our Brief Time in the Sun*.

Sebastien Doubinsky's charming *Is Poetry Contagious?* reveals the power of the arts to connect humanity. What if poetry were a virus? Just forty words, the poem is eloquent in its simplicity. Poet Marty Young finds solace in the act of creating, his poem, *An Endless Barrage*, testimony that engaging in the arts can provide a way to tame the chaos we find ourselves in. He writes: 'Only inside our creations / Where I can shelter from the carnage.' A connoisseur of horror, Young conjures nightmares to find his way whole.

While Young and others deliver proof that art and creativity can help us to make sense of the trauma and helplessness that currently plague us, the poems in *Infectious Hope* also offer a vital snapshot of this unprecedented period in world history, recording those 'undocumented delights' mentioned by Kat Clay in her insightful poem *Small Choices*. One day, presented with *Infectious Hope*, new generations might share in 'the act of reliving that reminiscence' (*Where Gulls Cry*, Anne Casey).

I'd like to take a moment to highlight two poems from *Infectious Hope* that resonated for me, personally. The first is Kyla Lee Ward's *Wardrobe Malfunction*. In this poem, which is couched in both whimsy and taffeta, the narrator explores the 'stygian depths' of their wardrobe, unable to find something suitable to wear to sit out the pandemic. In April of 2020, during New Zealand's lockdown, when the hospital offered me an unexpected opportunity to farewell my dying father, I felt this same irrational panic. What do you wear to the last time you'll see your father? I emptied my wardrobe, tried everything on. It was all wrong. In the end, I decided on something in red, the symbol of happiness and a colour my father loved to see me wear. (I needn't have bothered; even if Dad had been able to see me, PPE covered it all.)

The other poem which turned me inside out was Hester J. Rook's *the things that would not have happened, were it not for this*, and specifically her picture-perfect first stanza. I've read it several times now and cannot pass those lines without crying—not because it happened to me, but because it didn't.

No, no, this is unfair to the other poems. As a monster lover, how can I highlight those two and not mention Robert Hood's epic kaiju poem *The Ballad of the Monsters 2020*, or the truism of Dominic Hoey's piece, *They Only Become Dreams When You Wake*, with the dog that keeps running in its dreams? The thing is, the poems in this anthology are *all* my favourite, and this realisation brings me to an unexpected silver lining of the pandemic: this evocative book and its role in developing an exciting new anthologist-poet in editor Silvia Cantón Rondoni, who also released her own debut poetry collection, *Stark Naked*, in 2021. Under her gentle curatorship, and armed with the universal themes of hope, resilience, and creativity as a place of solace, Silvia has succeeded in coaxing extraordinary work from some of the world's most accomplished creatives. For a new poet, having the courage to approach your idols can be daunting enough, let alone undertaking the delicate task of shaping and ordering their work to give each poem its voice in the whole. To provide space for both quieter reflections and shrieks of frustration. To lead the reader on a journey through both the otherworldly and the familiar. With this anthology, Silvia has achieved her intent with grace, humility, and the 'sweet fluency' described by PS Cottier in speculative poem *Patterns*. *Infectious Hope* is a triumph, raising Silvia Cantón Rondoni to the ranks of world-class poet-anthologists.

Another small cause for hope.

Most importantly, though, this anthology is a means of holding space for those we love, and have loved, and for those loved ones who will survive us; Donna McLeod explains in her stunning powerhouse of a poem, *Ka whawhai tonu mātou*:

'*Āke, Ake, Ake!*' the poet writes in arresting, unshakeable *te reo Māori*.

Forever, evermore, forevermore.

Likewise, it is my hope that for you, as they have for me, the poems in *Infectious Hope* will linger long after you close its pages.

Lee Murray, March 2021

Preface To Infectious Hope
Silvia Cantón Rondoni, editor

Pandemic locked us in
and soon enough
we were out of hope, flour,
toilet rolls, family, milk.

It was then it dawned on me
how we continued to adapt
resilient to the new normal
unable to give up.

The world came to a stop
and we kept going,
living, loving, breathing,
holding onto each other tight.

Pandemics come around
once every hundred years
and we focus on the numbers,
what we lost, what's changed, what's wrong.

But what if we hoped
what if there was a cure for our fear
what if we all came together
and helped those who can't cope?

Let's create a batch of Infectious Hope
enough to supply the whole wide world
let's share what kept us going
so we are alone no more.

Linda D. Addison

BIO

Linda D. Addison is an award-winning author of five collections, including *The Place of Broken Things* written with Alessandro Manzetti, and *How To Recognize A Demon Has Become Your Friend*, recipient of the HWA Lifetime Achievement Award and SFPA Grand Master. Linda's website is: lindaaddisonpoet.com.

MOTIVATION

I believe reality/serenity exists in the present moment, not past memories or fearful futures.

HERE/NOW

Trying to gather lapsed moments,
  capturing shadows cast in
  benign, dimming memory.
  Nothing stays the same, not
wind, forest, the light passing through
window glass, nor voices echoing in
now empty rooms, all mis-remembered.

      Days yet-to-be, reflect in grey details,
       quivering in blurry darkness.
      Shapes unrecognizable by need
     for comfort /less illusion. Who can
    know songs not yet sung, flowers yet
    blooming, rain yet falling, stories yet
    told, within imagined, fragile spaces.

   The moment of one breath is infinite,
    within each inhale/exhale, born
    again & again. To be serene, relax
   here & discover fear, anxiety sensed,
  does not exist in the Now. As things break
  around us, we discover breakthroughs in the
hope of breath, of life shared with a changing world.

Ryka Aoki

BIO

Ryka Aoki is a poet, author, and composer who has been honored by the California State Senate for her "extraordinary commitment to free speech and artistic expression, as well as the visibility and well-being of Transgender people." She has an MFA in Creative Writing from Cornell University and is the recipient of a University Award from the Academy of American Poets. Her next novel, *Light from Uncommon Stars* is forthcoming from Tor Books in Fall 2021.

MOTIVATION

What if the resilience of our generations keeps us from naming and escaping our despair?

HUNGRY ONCE AGAIN, IN AMERICA,

I decided to risk another human
being here to bring me lettuce, milk, tuna fish,
bread. Last year I could have soft-boiled eggs
two and three at a time, could let
touch and taste, and tongue and teeth. Behind
my door, instead I checked my supplies
of canned meat, toilet paper, seaweed, rice. Like
Aunty after the war, great Aunty after the tsunami, great-
great Aunty after the famine... After,
someone suggested that I should read a book again,
practice an étude again. Burn some incense
down to ash and glean some Zen again. And yet
I'll blink, and 4000 souls will learn
to be quiet again. I'll blink and 4000 souls
will learn to be cold again, just as before
when we had our heartbeats, our heartbeats and more.

Our resilience, our patience, our silence—
pray for a vaccine against such pathogens. Pray
for an immunity that dances to cat hair, old underwear,
a week of dishes in the sink. Pray that this body be
convinced not to think, pray for the Buddha to say
fuck it, just fuck it, to say yes girl, yes, it's hopeless,
to knock on my door and say fuck the groceries,
let's make love—

Crisosto Apache

BIO

Crisosto Apache is originally from Mescalero, New Mexico (USA) on the Mescalero Apache Reservation, currently living in Denver, Colorado with his spouse. He is Mescalero, Chiricahua Apache, and Diné (Navajo). He holds an MFA from the Institute of American Indian Arts in Santa Fe, New Mexico. Crisosto's debut collection is called GENESIS *(Lost Alphabet)*.

MOTIVATION

Prayer is an important motivation for strength, wellness, and peace. Prayer also heals and has always been with us.

A PRAYER FOR US—
Ik ł'dá beedaajindánde

our song is sung to the eastern mountain.
our refrain remains inside a newborn
in spring chirping flickers push the quiet song
and we belong among the morning air

our song is sung toward the southern mountain
our youth in playful poise levels the afternoon
and heightens the yellow grasses, our children build
the frames of arbors holding the trees together

our song is sung to the western mountain
our drum beat demands consent of elders
to reflect the knowledge and hold better ways
of life that carve the strength in their voices

our song is sung to the northern mountain
our cries echo through looming slow fog
and waiting valleys as ash is spread on frozen grounds
to muffle the somber sighs and heavy sounds

Allen Ashley

BIO

Allen Ashley is an award-winning writer and editor based in London, UK. He works as a critical reader and a creative writing tutor. He is President of the British Fantasy Society.

MOTIVATION

An attempt to catch some of the multitude of feelings/emotions experienced during this pandemic.

SYMPTOMS MAY VARY

but could include:
feeling like you are falling… though very slowly.
Nostalgia for a life you never valued.
Vivid dreams, no dreams, thwarted dreams,
a new pendulum strain of claustrophobia and agoraphobia, flavoured
with a gag-inducing dose of anthropophobia.
Intense lethargy
—is there such a thing, is this a new variant?
The inability to distinguish today from any other
SunMonTue-WedBleughday .
Mood swings between despair and deflation.
Bouts of online shopping for items of dubious current value—hiking
boots, Samsonite luggage, swimming cossie—followed by cowering inside
when the delivery driver
rings the bell because you so fear human contact.
Solace in pets or baking, though not simultaneously.
A longing for the commute that demarcated home / work / home /work /
home /
working from home on call 24/7 Zoom fatigue leave me ALONE.
Wishing your "lost year" had been down to hedonistic living rather than
repeated lockdowns.
Acceptance, grudging acknowledgement, perhaps even a coming to terms.

I always said it was a happy ending if the lead character was alive at the
closing line—
stubborn survival
…Happy ending!

Eugen Bacon

BIO

Eugen Bacon is African Australian, a computer scientist mentally re-engineered into creative writing. Her work has won, been shortlisted and longlisted in awards, including the BSFA Award, Bridport Prize, Copyright Agency Prize, Australian Shadows Awards, Ditmar Awards and Nommo Award for Speculative Fiction by Africans. Website: eugenbacon.com Twitter: @EugenBacon.

MOTIVATION

My epigraphs in 2020 chimed longing, unsettlement and rage—it was refreshing to chart hopefulness.

WHAT THE MASK SAW

the mask whirls before restrictions
her string and feather wings pirouette to a ditty
of human truths engorged with antibodies flouting type-1 activity
she takes to incandescent
skies gazes at the glimmer of a man with naked feet buying roses
snapdragons proteas delphiniums so a florist can keep aloft ahead of
lockdown five mouths to feed
a sign at the supermarket says elderly only
a neon at a vacant mall dusty with sunset rugs broadcasts quarantine bingo
free penguin parade on a virtual bridge

the mask hip-hops to opera live streaming a sonorous eloquence of the
cello
a silvery melancholy of the flute
a solemn transcendence of the oboe a rippling wave
in loops of the violin playing dante all the way to paradise on the other side

the mask perceives a post box painted blue
emblazoned in white across his chest
saying thank you first responders
studies the corner shop meting hand sanitisers to
a food bank   discerns clapping   the city's applause for carers
lauds to hearten ventilators tubes monitors pumps in a frost-white icu
she trembles with a bride in an off-shoulder mermaid-scoop whose groom
has no aisle runner no reserved seating   just a ring pillow unity candle
and silk rose petals   they say i do on a zoom wedding thronged with
strangers from the cork of the universe in a quickyear

the mask sees hope is a realm shifting patients to ocean
breaks   quintessential
rainbows   concealed kindness of strangers / resilience is a diamond planet
adorning love across its balconies   gladdening lakes in a pink shimmer of
flamingos irradiating the waters / future is the first day of school after eons
of piano in iso   an amity of campaigners hooking elbows with coppers
bending knees on newfound lands that closely resemble earth

Esther Belin

BIO

Esther Belin, a Diné writer and artist, won the American Book Award for her first book of poetry, *From the Belly of My Beauty* in 2000. Her second book, *Of Cartography*, was published in 2017. She is currently an MFA faculty mentor at the Institute of American Indian Arts.

MOTIVATION

How to work through life's challenges slowly and with intent.

WASHING DISHES IS GOOD MEDICINE

The scene out the window has changed over the years—some years—there was no window – only a wall.

The process always remains the same, like blindly diving into a wreck with only your hands. I generally like to wash dishes without gloves and feel my way around the hotter than warm sudsy water.

Though my current home has a lovely spacious sink, there have been many years where I longed for a deep and wide sink to hold all the mess needing cleaning. A place able to cover over life's messes where only the foaming crust of dish soap alluded to a full and busy life. A place I felt gratitude toward the steamy water and detergent silently doing their job of loosening grime and softening hard-bent residue of daily existence.

Sometimes I just stand over the sink full of dishes and soak my thoughts clean, rinse them, scrub them rough-handed, disposing debris drippings, like over-boiled bone soup, slowly inching, slowly reaching into yesterday's pitfalls, today's nonverbal discontent and tomorrow's threats like a curdling warm thaw relaxing the chill in my blood, regulating the beat in my rhythmic dunking and squeezing the sponge of life-giving joy. Washing dishes is good medicine. Caked and burnt on outer layers are ladled off and out and eventually tunnel down the drain, buried in the depths of the earth.

Yes, washing dishes is good medicine.

Jenny Blackford

BIO

Jenny's poems and stories have appeared in Going Down Swinging, Westerly and many more Australian and international journals and anthologies. Her second children's novel from Christmas Press is due in May 2021. Pitt Street Poetry published her third poetry collection, *The Alpaca Cantos*, in March 2020, just in time for lockdown.

MOTIVATION

My priority throughout the pandemic has been my father's safety.

THE DANCE

Even when shelves bulged with toilet rolls, I stalked the aisles
glaring like a snake-haired Gorgon at the careless:
I'll kill you if you risk my father's life. The small machine
that shocks him gently every time his heart forgets
reminds me beat by beat how fragile we all are,
even him, the lucky last alive of thirteen country kids.

The weekend of the first false dawn, kids
out of home confinement shouted screamed and raced
along the supermarket corridors touching everything
and everyone, sniffling and coughing, parents pretending
not to know them. I hissed with fury by the time
I pushed my disinfected trolley to the car, rubbing
my scaly hands with yet more smelly gel.

Fiercer lockdowns, more false dawns. Dad's happily alive,
thank all the gods. After his lunch today the traffic
was insane, mostly hi-vis blokes in utes rushing
towards the long weekend, but once indoors
the supermarket dance flowed graceful, easy,
filled with smiles and excuse-mes and after-yous
as all the shoppers twirled and do-si-doed
and reeled their carts aside,
a care-filled metre and a half or two apart
as if we'd done it all our whirling lives.

Isobelle Carmody

BIO

Isobelle Carmody is an award-winning writer of more than thirty novels for young people and adults. She also illustrated several of her books for younger readers. She completed a PhD in 2020 and is currently working in a novel called *The Theatre of Death*. Her latest novel is *The Velvet City*.

MOTIVATION

A friend told me she worried about what would become of the chickens people got for comfort during COVID.

THE CHICKENS OF THE APOCALYPSE

When an apocalypse looms, the movies
cut to action. They don't show the before:
the great restless wind that blows through,
the way light burns greenish, turns faces
sick; casts doubt; the way apprehension
opens an abyss and if you don't fall for it
or jump, how you can mask terror
and boredom mulching, weeding,
kneading. Seek refuge in baking.

Others hatch eggs, take comfort
in the marvellous down, the swift
stubborn beat of life growing
in its house of feathers. Watch Netflix, one hand
masterful on the chicken you named Courage,
thinking one twist is all it would take.
Listening for darker wings.

And when it ends before the end,
books tell the climax but not the confusion.
Minor characters in the aftermath
staggering out of isolation, wondering
if life can just go on, after all that.

A journalist once told me, after,
surviving disaster, some folk just walk
out of their lives, as through a door.

Jay Caselberg

BIO

Jay Caselberg is an Australian author and poet based in Europe. His work, poetry, short stories, and novels, has appeared around the world and been translated into several languages. From time to time, it gets shortlisted for awards. He can be found at caselberg.net

MOTIVATION

All hardship is transformative in one way or another. Sometimes transformation is an aspect of growth.

CHRYSALIS

The burning and this pestilence
Plough furrowed brows
Scored deep
Weeping now a flood
Still gone the multitude
But unforgotten yet
They linger

Action in this isolation
No touch, no feel
The passions gone
And exiled
A realm limned with anger
Closed fingers
Stirring solitudes alone

As bound with cloth and shroud like
Wrapped tight with wings
Stretching for a lightness
Once assumed
Cocoon walls then riven
Mere husk behind
      See there what gleams ahead

Anne Casey

BIO

A journalist, magazine editor, legal author and media communications director for 30 years, Anne Casey is an award-winning Irish poet/writer living in Australia. Author of two collections, *out of emptied cups* and *where the lost things go*, her work is widely published internationally, ranking in The Irish Times #39 Most Read.

MOTIVATION

This poem captures my heartache for my native west of Ireland as an immigrant exiled in Australia in the time of COVID.

WHERE GULLS CRY

I could tell you how the whole earth seems to end
at this one place where the land falls
cleanly into a tumultuous thundering—
the relentless roar of furious millennia crashing
iced cobalt against three hundred million years
of vertical bituminous siltstone stubbornness,
all overlaid with a violence of vivid greenness
inconceivable until witnessed, where the sky splits
open above-brewing caliginous charcoal yielding
to an inevitability of iridescence, streaming
shards spearing simmering drizzle-laden mists,
all lit as if from within with an otherworldly luminosity
approximating divinity, a scene so sharp yet ethereal,
surreal, imprinted in a part of self within but apart
that might burst from this pulsing bone-suit, this
shadow-world flesh-mantle sheerly in the act
of reliving that reminiscence. I could tell you
all of that or I could say how much this exiled

soul aches for home.

Kat Clay

BIO

Kat Clay is an award-winning genre fiction author from Melbourne, Australia. Her short story *Lady Loveday Investigates* won three prizes at the 2018 Scarlet Stilettos, including the Kerry Greenwood Prize for best malice domestic. She is the author of *Double Exposure*, and her work has been published in Aurealis, Weird Fiction Review, and Crimson Streets.

MOTIVATION

I was trying to express the feeling of being in Melbourne's lockdown—how hard it was, but also the small reminders of joy I discovered during this time.

SMALL CHOICES

Where will you spend your hour of freedom?
> Past palm tree and riverside, an illicit three minutes over the hour, or —
> Free wheeling to a nameless park, 5kms from your home.
> Life shrinks. So do choices.

Small decisions—
> Lounge room or balcony.
> North Face or suit.
> Uber Eats or Deliveroo.

These choices slowly turn inwards, curling as a Fibonacci spiral,
> as you are faced with yourself sans schedule, sans socialisation.

Make a choice for which tears you will cry today—
> Left eye or right
> For your mother or your sister
> Or the distance between you all.

And in the sadness you choose to notice small things—
> Cut of spring light on a cherry blossom tree.
> Waggle of tail in the doggoe park parade.
> Hi-vized council workers singing songs, sanitising poles.

> For freedom is as much as in a space as in the mind.

A lockdown prayer: Remind us of these undocumented delights—
> Ice cream slurped as a mask dangles from one ear
> Wind on your cycle at the sea
> Hug from a friend you've held at elbow's length out of love.

Let these small choices guide our lives from here—joy in all things and not despair.
> And ask yourself, always:
> > Where will you spend your life of freedom?

Claire G. Coleman

BIO

Claire G. Coleman is a Noongar woman whose ancestral country is on the south coast of Western Australia. She writes fiction, non-fiction and verse while living in Naarm or traveling around the continent in a caravan. She is the author of two novels and a non-fiction book, *Lies, Damned Lies* (Ultimo Press, 2021).

MOTIVATION

I live by a river, and rivers are where I find comfort, yet the river is not mine.

I CANNOT SING WITH THE RIVER

The river sings
And it does not know how to stop
Ands I am trying
To remember how to listen
And I cannot hear myself crying

The river sings and
My head feels like an apocalypse
I give my breath to the water
And the water has no need
But keeps it regardless

The river sings and I
Want to sing along voiceless
But this is not my river
Yet I know she welcomes me
My heart falls broken bleeding

The river sings and I know
The song of the river is not mine
But I know she sings it for
Me regardless
Me, non-exclusive.

The river sings and I know I
Am far from Boodjar
From my own river
I want to go home
Ask the river, "take me there"

PS Cottier

BIO

PS Cottier is a poet based in Canberra. Her poetry appears in numerous journals and anthologies, and in 2014 she edited *The Stars Like Sand: Australian Speculative Poetry* with Tim Jones. In 2020 she had two books published: *Monstrous* (Interactive Press) and *Utterly* (Ginninderra Press). PS Cottier wrote a PhD on images of animals in the works of Charles Dickens, and is Poetry Editor at the Canberra Times.

MOTIVATION

The idea that something long-lasting, based on often undervalued skills, could begin during a crisis inspired *Patterns*.

PATTERNS

2020

She breaks out some long-stored fabric,
eighties funk splotched in mauve and gold.
Intended for a party dress,
the party somehow never came.
She sews masks, slow at first,
then sweet fluency breaks out.
She gives them to strangers,
when and where she can.

2030

The patchwork grows, coral slow.
One day it will be unfurled, particoloured,
one square for each local lost back then.
She works with two more women,
and their hands, age-blotched and skilled
form this bright remembrance.
The survivors sit and chat and sew.
Armed with needles, The Three Masketeers .

Cardinal Cox

BIO

Cardinal Cox's career includes being Poet-in-Residence of The Dracula Society (2015-2017). This led to both his one-man "spooken word" show *High Stakes* (that was performed at World SF Conventions in both Helsinki and Dublin) and his second collection *Grave Goods*, released by Demain Publications. Likes cake.

MOTIVATION

Even if we inhabit a nihilistic universe, hope can make the present temporally bearable.

BEFORE THE DAWN

Poisonous eyes shining at night—Graph's curve escalating upwards
Shadow of taloned hand extending towards innocence
After every longest night Sun crawls over horizon
Peeping through freezing fog—stark trees in silhouette
Spring's first green shoots struggling against winter's
Greys—recall ice-age's forgotten long-centuries thaw
Tyrants in tarnished palaces grow feeble—advisors desert
Aids abscond with treasure—taxi to airport ahead of mob
Scientists reveal formulae—collaboratively developed
Internationally—to defeat saucer-piloting aliens
Peasants roused from rough hovels armed with agricultural
Implements surround the monster's redoubt
Flash-bulbs nova on courthouse steps drench
Detective as he announces his satisfaction at sentence
Bowie knife held high above farm cart's casket
Swift arc and it ploughs Vampire's withered throat
Frantic flint chipping—dry grass nest of sparks
The branch held aloft—night's unseen denizens flee
Beside grave we remember brave soldier—innocent bystander
Those who couldn't flee - Those who fell—we remember
But we stand—the damaged—the survivors—but all
The victorious—to say we won—we will win again

Jack Dann

BIO

Jack Dann is a multi-award winning author who has written or edited over seventy-five books, including the international bestseller *The Memory Cathedral*, *The Rebel*, *The Silent*, and *The Man Who Melted*. His latest novel is *Shadows in the Stone*. Forthcoming is a *Centipede Press Masters of Science Fiction* volume.

MOTIVATION

The poem suddenly appeared as a visual image while talking with my publisher about book scheduling in the time of COVID.

HOUSE ARREST

Another big blue eye gazing through my window
6:30 sunshine
Blue blue sky and pupiled clouds
All iris

Another wake-up morning
Another bleary, blue-eyed morning
Another winter autumn spring summer morning
Another COVID morning

The daylight days pass like frost at the farm
Cold warm quiet stormy gale-force days
Each month day hour minute second
Different yet maddeningly the same

I look forward to the past
Remember the future
And somehow with great sadness
Forget the present

Sebastien Doubinsky

BIO

Sebastien Doubinsky is a bilingual French fiction writer and poet, born in 1963. His novels and poetry collections are published in France, USA and the UK.

MOTIVATION

To kick both poetry and COVID from their pedestals in one go.

IS POETRY CONTAGIOUS?

Is poetry contagious?
Can you catch poetry by shaking hands?
Should poetry be confined?
Does poetry imply drone-surveillance?
Is poetry socially distancing?
Do we need to wash hands after having touched poetry?
Can the world be normal again after poetry?

Nigel Ellis

BIO

Nigel Ellis is an Australian poet, musician, and writer. He has been published in various journals and collections in Australia and abroad. His poetry often concerns his fascination with liminal spaces. His debut collection *Haematograms* was published in 2012 by Neopoiesis Press.

MOTIVATION

It seems to me that we've never been so concerned about breathing. Of course, to breathe is to live. Metaphorically, it is life-affirming, regenerative. And in pause we can find peace.

IN THE TIME OF BREATHING

we rise. Let
open windows. Faces
moonlike sunlike bloomlike rise
From beds we rise and
walk to windows

in the time of breathing
this wind opens this window
pens this time holds
this favourite hour when
we mingle breath
in the evening
in the morning

we rise

in the sheets a scent like leavened bread
in the time of breathing

Stephanie Ellis

BIO

Stephanie Ellis is a published writer and poet. Her poetry has been included in the *HWA's Poetry Showcase Volume 6* and 7 and in the online zine *Visual Verse*. She has two collections of dark poetry, *The Art of Dying* and *Dark is my Playground*, available on Amazon.

MOTIVATION

Another Eve was written in protest at the language of fear used during the pandemic.

ANOTHER EVE

She swallowed an apple that spring
Gazed out from coffined panes
At empty streets, barren of princes
Bare of laughter

Became afraid
Of the parade
Of numbers

Numbed at the view
Of a future
Gone

On and on,
This relentless hammering
Of nails
Pinned her down
A butterfly
On a frozen wheel

Until she rebelled
Denied despair
Smashing her windows
Another Eve
Breaking the rule of fear

Better to walk on broken glass
Than hide behind it

Rebecca Fraser

BIO

Rebecca Fraser is an award-nominated Australian author who writes genre-mashing fiction for both children and adults. To provide her muse with life's essentials, Rebecca copywrites and edits in a freelance capacity, however her true passion lies in storytelling. Say G'day at writingandmoonlighting.com Facebook @writingandmoonlighting or Twitter/Insta @becksmuse.

MOTIVATION

To hold a mirror up to society's ugliness, yet also reflect back hope.

#breathe

Planes grounded in the suffocating desert—
a school of microlattice fish, tail fins glinting
in the corona-ringed sun, hinting
Of memories—the breathless thrill of flight, when we could take to the sky...
(Zoom Zoom Zoom) Take yourself off mute, reboot
#itsnotforever #wereallinthistogether we cry,
Then why
Beneath a star-spangled sky, a black man pleaded (unheeded)
#icantbreathe No reprieve
for the oppressed, where voices aren't suppressed
By masks alone
(Look at my mask. It's a Banksy design. Isn't it woke?)
#isthatajoke
It's suffocating... Wake up!
To a pandemic-cleansed dawn where kindness is more than talk,
And rainbows and butterflies drawn in chalk.
Wash your hands (for at least twenty seconds)
Of conspiracy theories and other viral contagion
Wrestle off your ventilator (hater),
No artificial ~~breathing~~ thinking required.
Fill your lungs and mind and heart,
Restart.
Unfurl your desert-scorched wings and
#breathe

Owl Goingback

BIO

Owl Goingback is the author of numerous novels, a children's book, screenplays, magazine articles, and short stories. He is a HWA Lifetime Achievement Award Recipient, a two-time Bram Stoker Award ® winner, and a Nebula Award Nominee. His books include *Crota, Darker Than Night, Evil Whispers, Breed, Shaman Moon, Coyote Rage, Eagle Feathers, Tribal Screams*, and *The Gift*.

MOTIVATION

My mother died from COVID. Her name was Quiet Starr.

QUIET STARS

She died alone.
Visitors forbidden, her hand unheld.
Just another ticker tape number
in a pandemic lottery.

Beyond her hospital window,
the streets lie empty.
Where lovers once walked,
only shadows parade.

In abiding darkness, despair.
Children cry out for parents lost,
while husbands weep for wives no more.
Nations once proud, bow before COVID gods.

And the wealthy hide
behind walls of broken promises,
clutching rolls of tissue
to their gilded chests.

A million departed souls pass
like fireflies in the night,
lifting up to light the sky
like quiet stars.

Glittery points of faraway light,
names on Death's sacred scroll.
Spirits now to guide us,
before our final bell tolls.

Oz Hardwick

BIO

Oz Hardwick is a European poet, photographer, musician and academic who has published nine collections and chapbooks. His chapbook *Learning to Have Lost* (Canberra: IPSI, 2018) won the 2019 Rubery International Book Award for poetry, and his most recent publication is the prose poetry sequence *Wolf Planet* (Clevedon: Hedgehog, 2020).

MOTIVATION

Shopping for essentials is the new Big Night Out. We're all dancers under the skin.

THE TROCADERO SHOPPING MALL

Supermarkets have become nightclubs, with rope
barriers and slate-faced men in black ties. Their aisles
have become playgrounds for Premier League
footballers and stars of soaps and reality TV, with
rumours of tomatoes and hand sanitizer piled like
stalagmites in fantastic caves. The air is germ-free
and beautiful. Muzak winds solitary waltzers through
the glow of freezers, distanced partners responding
to each minute gesture, each twinkle in longing eyes.
If your name's not on the list you could wait for
days, your heart pressed to toughened glass,
reconsidering what's essential, as the smug and lucky
stuff bags-for-life with starfruit, avocado and
prosecco, arranging clandestine tête-à-têtes for the
endless weekends. By the time they let you in,
checking your i.d. with bored suspicion, the music
has stopped and the shelves are empty. Someone
hands you a mop and a candle stub, then turns off
the lights.

Dominique Hecq

BIO

Dominique Hecq grew up in the French-speaking part of Belgium. She now lives in Melbourne. Hecq writes across genres and disciplines—and sometimes across tongues. Her creative works include a novel, three collections of stories, and ten volumes of poetry. *Kaosmos* and *Tracks* are her latest collections.

MOTIVATION

I wrote this piece in response to the sudden lock down of housing commission towers in Flemington on July 4th 2020.

FIVE DAYS IN FOUR HUNDRED WORDS

They have locked down the poor people: refugees, immigrants, disabled people, disenfranchised citizens. Corella sees all this on the telly. She squirms. She'd gladly pour herself a wine, but doesn't. She watches masked police officers swarm her screen. The man begging for formula to feed his newborn. The teenager screaming that she's run out of medication. The woman who can't speak English. Corella feels dizzy. She notes that the rapid evolution of events is due to Corona's physical virus and mental viral activity. Corella dons a rainbow mask. Says one works by conferring freedom of anonymity and enabling projection. It liberates the wearer from caged emotions like pain or anger, above all, confusion. Because she rubbishes ideological positions posturing as social criticism, her mask's underside is blackened. She waits behind a glass door, texting the crows and ravens of the neighbourhood, curious to see whether she'll be charged with violation of taboo, which incurs social and religious restraint, then censure. Corella waits. She goes shopping. Long queues outside the supermarket. She avails herself of the hand sanitiser on entering the store. Notices the dispensing staff wears no mask. She packs eggs, milk and minced meat in her basket. No more than the allowed quantities. Dog biscuits, tea, coffee. Broccoli, carrots, potatoes, apples, oranges. As she unpacks her items, Corella has a brain wave: the face mask may be a symbol for social responsibility but also for muting, de-identification, profiling, anonymity. She wakes to the guttural squawks of wattle birds and calls of magpies. Geopolitics, scandals, petty crimes, local polemics, yesterday's fatalities and sports on the news. The weather is the new black. Prickly Pear and Arum Lily pose a serious threat to Corella's suburb. She should take an active interest in the urban reaches of the Creek in her backyard. No mention of poor people's fate, except in countries where floods and landslides are sweeping them dead. Corella googles 'towers' and 'lockdown'. The poor people's towers stand still, masked in grey, oblivious to all waiting for their Corona test results. There are police check-points amid wattle bursting into bloom on the side of ring roads, arteries, avenues, and dead ends upon which the towers spire on, their internal air circulation whirring, heating humming, lifts at a stand-still. Waiting has smothered the babies' screams. The children's nagging. Wind blows. Five long sad notes. Repeat. The measure of a human heart beating.

Dominic Hoey

BIO

Dominic Hoey is a playwright, poet and novelist based in Auckland. He's traveled the world performing his spoken word poetry. He has a vicious pomeranian named Prince Chilli, and wastes his spare time daydreaming about a post-capitalist world.

MOTIVATION

This poem was inspired by the dream-like quality of lockdown, and spending too much time in my bed.

THEY ONLY BECOME DREAMS
WHEN YOU WAKE

someone much wiser than me
once called her bed an all purpose venue
this is the year of sleep
stay warm
watching history dry on my phone

my dog suspects nothing
we are in step now
eat
walk
sleep
repeat
reduce life to its bones
and yet the days still pass
like drunk drivers

behind my mask i am laughing
everything dangerous and ridiculous
the dog keeps running in its dreams
but we are going nowhere

Robert Hood

BIO

Robert Hood is an award-winning author of horror, crime, weird fiction and SF. His work includes novels such as *Fragments of a Broken Land: Valarl Undead*, over 150 short stories, collections (including *Peripheral Visions: The Collected Ghost Stories*), children's books, literary articles and plays. More info at roberthoodwriter.com.

MOTIVATION

As a monster aficionado, I found that a monster battle for supremacy described 2020 rather well.

THE BALLAD OF THE MONSTERS 2020

after disruptive Fire
born of the Climate (ever
mutating in response to
Careless Evil), there comes
the rise of a new Terror,
an invader of Human flesh
that closes down normality,
brings death to some and
annoying hardship to many.

this new Terror gives birth to
Isolation, a virus-driven Monster
rampaging across civil (and uncivil)
Human society, forcing even
more domesticated monsters—
Godzilla, Kong and 007 among them—
to cringe in fear and hide
from the once-ruling Schedule
(born of the monster Capitalism).

worldwide, Humans struggle on,
mourning the dead, developing
weapons to beat the invisible
Monsters within them, and
meditating on the question:

which Monster rules the planet
and will claim what's left of it…
in the end?

Roz Kaveney

BIO

Roz Kaveney is a poet, novelist, critic and activist living in London. Her *Selected Poems* are published in September 2021.

MOTIVATION

My poetry has always been about fragility and transience. *Persist* is typical of my themes.

PERSIST

Live all your great good times as if one day
Particular remembered is a scene
In someone's novel or the flash of green
In that girl's eyes is echoed in the way

Leaves glisten on a canvas by the son
Who watched her die.
They wind from joy or pain
The stuff that makes us die or live again
Become the thread whose weaving's just begun

Echo through makers' minds a thousand years.
Deserted lover's spite.
The choral praise
Of mother goddess.
All the discord ways
We whisper laugh.
Griefs ecstasies and fears.

We die soap bubble snap. Yet single frame
Persists shines treasured without face or name.

Joe R. Lansdale

BIO

Joe R. Lansdale is the author of fifty novels and four hundred shorter works, including stories, essays, reviews, film and TV scripts, introductions, and magazine articles. His work has been made into films, *Bubba Hotep*, *Cold in July*, as well as the acclaimed TV show, *Hap and Leonard*. He has also had works adapted to *Masters of Horror On Showtime*, and wrote scripts for *Batman The Animated Series*, and *Superman The Animated Series*. He scripted a special *Jonah Hex* animated short, as well as the animated Batman film, *Son of Batman*. He has also written scripts for John Irvin, John Wells, and Ridley Scott, as well as the Sundance TV show based on his work, *Hap and Leonard*. His novel, *The Thicket*, is set to film in the near future, and will star Peter Dinklage. He has received numerous recognitions and awards for his work.

MOTIVATION

I hate to give an answer that sounds flip, because it isn't flip, but I woke up in a good mood, and remembered some of the bad moods during the pandemic, a kind of malaise I wore like a cheap suit with a grease stain on the pocket. The grease was gone, and the suit was new, and like in the poem, I had a good cup of coffee. The poem slipped out.

THE MOMENT PASSES

Disease floats by my window as I look out
thinking its waiting for me in the wilds of the land
on the air
on a pear
on fingers and hands washed red
with consternation and iron-heavy tap water
I think I must mask in the shower
mask in the hall
mask at night when I play with my balls
mask up the dog, the cat, the rats in the wall
the roaches wearing tiny masks by the thousands
heavens don't forget the wasps in the garage
a nest full of buzzers ready to dive
they need masks too
and then the clouds roll out
and the sun rolls in
and on my porch
less fearful
my mask in my pocket
I am not scared of anything
My heart has left on a happy rocket
and a dark roast cup of coffee
no cream

Steph Lum

BIO

Steph Lum is an Australian intersex advocate and poet. Stephanie is the founder and editor of YOUth&I, an anthology by young intersex people, and has recently moved to Ireland to study a PhD on intersex legal reform. Stephanie's works have been published in the *Australian Poetry Anthology* and *Not Very Quiet*.

MOTIVATION

Moving during a pandemic trapped me. Routine became survival.

RECREATE

0600   Mornings
0700   Get up sit down look out the window
0800   In my new life
0900   Routines have replaced people
1000   I don't know why now
1100   I've become a morning person
1200   Now I have endless days
1300   Third lockdown third city
1400   Different moods different people
1500   Different routines
1600   The first felt like purpose
1700   The second like observer
1800   This time I'm alone and the mood is
1900   Laughter that has nowhere to go
2000   A picture of a coffee cup on a Zoom call
2100   Shoes still in suitcase
2200   Get up sit down look out the window
2300   I like to sit on my windowsill
0000   Over red bricked buildings and black tiled roofs
0100   Over a city I don't yet know
0200   Over people I'm yet to meet
0300   Get up sit down look out the window
0400   And just like that
0500   Another day goes by

Alessandro Manzetti

BIO

Alessandro Manzetti (Rome, Italy) is a two-time Bram Stoker Award® and SFPA Elgin Award winning author, editor, scriptwriter and essayist of horror fiction and dark poetry. He has published more than 40 books, including *Naraka, Whitechapel Rhapsody, The Place of Broken Things* (with Linda D. Addison), *Eden Underground*. Website: battiago.com.

MOTIVATION

Isolation is like a prison, but our inner world is bigger than a planet.

WHEN SHE LEFT

When Madame Hope left
I felt so still for weeks
like a tine soldier, with welded feet
on a so little piece of ground.

The crocodile of my anguish
shrunk, toothless, tamed
on a bourgeois fat lady's leash,
stared at me laughing.

Then a boy with a reddish face
threw me into the fray;
his little battle screaming
on a Persian rug in the dining room.

I raised my rifle over the trench edge.
and saw my Madame again, up there
a thousand miles above my thoughts
with the North Star stuck in her navel.

All I had to do was open my eyes,
she never left, she never turned out the light,
and now I'm walking like a crazy king,
wearing my new leopard cloak,
on the endless avenues of myself
laughing at prisons and laws of physics.

Kirstyn Mcdermott

BIO

Kirstyn McDermott is the author of two novels, *Madigan Mine* and *Perfections*, as well as a short fiction collection, *Caution: Contains Small Parts*. She produces and co-hosts *The Writer and the Critic*, a literary discussion podcast, and recently completed a PhD with a focus on creative writing and fairy tales. Website: kirstynmcdermott.com.

MOTIVATION

I sought to capture a fleeting emotional snapshot of 2020 which might otherwise be lost.

UNTOUCHED

On your pantry shelf
swaddled in bright metallic blue
squats the most expensive kilo of flour you've ever owned
      you've killed two sourdough starters already
      never made those hot cross buns
            face it you're not a baker and yet:
struck by panic or perhaps a streak of contrary ambition
      you bought the last bag standing
      and still it stands   untouched
          awaiting the recipe you both deserve.

You don't know all their names but this one
barrelling towards you from the other side of the dog park
      tongue lolling in welcome
      coat grey-blue like her namesake is Luna
social distancing a foreign concept to hounds and novel to you
      so you hesitate: *wait, what are the rules*?   too late:
her body thumps against your legs in hard tail-driven joy
      your hands pressing into flanks sun-warmed and soft
          a touch as vital as the breath expanding her ribs
          and you don't mean to cry   but you do.

One day you will write a poem
just to feel its fur ripple beneath your palms:
      shiny and blue as a kept promise.

Donna McLeod

BIO

Donna McLeod lives on Papakāinga surrounded by *whānau* in Motueka. As Manawhenua she feels blessed to live within tribal and *marae* lands. She is a poet, actor and playwright with Te Oro Haa and a member of Te Ohu Whakaari.

MOTIVATION

Ka whawhai tonu mātou is the reality for us as Māori in Aotearoa. Knowing that COVID will decimate our people but deep within we refuse to go lightly. *Moko kauae* is resistance.

Ka whawhai tonu mātou

My Nanny spoke of her father, a child of Parihaka.
Standing beside children offering bread, singing, skipping
before 2000 invading, armed soldiers

My Nanny spoke of the 1918's influenza.
Awaking to mourn, awaiting the cart collecting their dead.

My Nanny never spoke of TB taking her children.

My Nanny held their space.
Her unspoken reverberates
in us, her Mokopuna, her reflection.

My Nanny's long ago "God Bless"
holds my Mokopuna, children and I in 2020.

I reflect on One Tree Hill's obelisk to our extinction.

Yesterday my sisters upheld their chins
to the artist's drill's, chiselled heartbeat,
incisions of fine blue ancient lines of our nannies.

Reclaiming, regrounding, redirecting.
Boundless blood blue lines.

Moko kauae, soul lines reflecting tomorrow's hope

As their children's children read the lines,
tracing with fingertips, now caught in their dreams.
They speak. They hold. We reverberate. We live.

Our mokopuna. Our reflection
A child, boundless hope

Ake! Ake! Ake!

Fiona Murphy

BIO

Fiona Murphy is a deaf poet and essayist, based in Australia. Her memoir, *The Shape of Sound*, is out now through Text Publishing.

MOTIVATION

In a year that has been both chaotic and mundane, our attention has turned towards the dailiness of our lives. This intense focus invites complex questions such as: Happy?

PERPETUAL STASIS

Stunned by the heat, we squander the day,
entombed in a drape drawn room.

Sweat pools in the creases of our knees
sticking hair to skin.

The sofa springs whine as Martha shifts
from cheek to cheek, flapping her skirt before changing the channel.

> The southern border will close from midnight tonight. The northern
> border remains shut until further notice. Expect the heatwave to
> continue until Friday. Possible showers Saturday morning.

Change the channel, yeah? There must be something better on, you know?

> They're all the same, she says.

After another ad break: click. She turns off the television.
The room is dark and quiet and still.

> Happy?

Jason Nahrung

BIO

Jason Nahrung is a Ballarat-based journalist, editor and writer. He is the author of four novels and more than 20 short stories, all within the speculative fiction genre. He has a PhD in creative writing from The University of Queensland focused on climate fiction. Jason's website is: jasonnahrung.com.

MOTIVATION

The COVID lockdown has illustrated how we can change our behaviours to benefit Earth.

GROUNDED

clear skies
the only zooming done on screen
breathing deeply
seeing
stars
mountains
for the first time in an industrial age
we rediscover trees.
art.
each other.

See:

we can do this.

Biola Olatunde

BIO

I am a writer, poet and television producer. I have written and produced for international and national agencies on social issues. I still write.

MOTIVATION

My motivation for writing the poem is the growing desperation for humanity to have an answer to the menace of the pandemic.

THE UNBUCKLING

The headache made the lightning journey
Across a seared forehead
He gasped from a blocked throat of phlegm
A temperature of hell
They said it was COVID
He counted his days
And prayed for help
The masquerades also prayed
To stop the corona stampede
Of human souls to the ancients
No more stools for the dead
Longed for freshness
Like the love aglow
In his heart
His spirit limp
He kept the social distance
Six feet apart they said
Like the six feet under
The door opened
I am hope she said
Here is the vaccine
The dawn came
And life returned.

Yenn Purkis

BIO

Yenn Purkis is an autistic and non-binary author, public speaker and community leader with a diagnosis of schizophrenia. Yenn has written eight published books and is a regular blogger. Yenn was the 2016 ACT Volunteer of the Year and won the 2019 ACT Chief Minister's Inclusion Award. Yenn has also presented at TEDx Canberra.

MOTIVATION

A reflection on hope and personal growth in a challenging time.

A HAPPY THOUGHT

Einstein's happy thought saw space and time dancing in beauty and logic
My happy thought not earth-shattering yet also monumental
A monument to health and life
A prize of insight and wisdom
'Imagine if in six months that all will be well'
Nonsense when I dreamed it into existence
At the time of thinking it my sorry self was ensconced in the psychiatric ward
Depression and psychosis my constant companions
Comrades in an unholy war
Doubt far outweighing certainty
Yet here it is, that happy thought
'In six months time I will look back and know that it all worked out OK'

Somehow, impossibly the happy thought was right
It IS all OK
Hardly credible, inexplicably true
My mind is calm - mostly
Each morning I dance in front of the bedroom mirror
Endless gratitude for the implausible change in my fate
Yes, my happy thought changed the world
Not the vast majesty of space-time seen by Einstein
But my own deep inner space
Majestic in its own way
A happy thought come to fruition
I sing for the joy and the wonder of my thought becoming reality

Dan Rabarts

BIO

Dan Rabarts is an award-winning poet, editor and author of dark fantasy, science fiction and horror novels and short stories, living in Porirua, Aotearoa New Zealand. Find out more about his work at dan.rabarts.com.

MOTIVATION

From the relative safety of our islands, we hurt alongside the world beyond our borders.

DISJOINTED

Now we breathe

                              Choke down the violence

Reach out

                                 Across the borders

Knowing this microscopic sting

                                    A fragile thing

So perfect, so deadly can be

                                    Life or death

Overcome

                           By our hands, apart we stand

With compassion

                    What black magic has nature wrought

This liminal space

                                Where we fought

We survived

                  For isolation from this burning man

The ash on our lips so bitter

             Why will he not understand the ripples of choice

This freedom

             These circles of pain are mine and yours and his

Providence of oceans

                        Our personal apocalypse

And barring of doors

       Each of us soldiers in this invisible, impossible war.

Hester J. Rook

BIO

Hester J. Rook is an Australian Shadows Award-winning and Rhysling Award-shortlisted poet, fiction writer and co-editor of Twisted Moon Magazine. They are often found salt-scrunched on beaches, reading arcane tales and losing the moon in mugs of tea. Find Hester on Twitter @hesterjrook Read more poems and fiction at hesterjrook.com.

MOTIVATION

There've been precious things, amongst the bad, we must hold on tight.

the things that would not have happened, were it not for this

1. steam, fogged like breath against the webcam, the hiss and sizzle of frying vegetables, here, tilt the camera, the dumpling skins should be this thin, careful they do not stick, here, we laugh and hunger, burnt mouths and warm hearts and a border between us

2. a treasure hunt (or three), X marks the spot, here is your map, I have hidden my gift in the sprawl of nasturtiums, the proud branches of grevillea stand guard, hurry, it waits for you

3. a treasure hunt (or three), X marks the spot, here is your map, I have hidden my gift in the sprawl of nasturtiums, the proud branches of grevillea stand guard, hurry, it waits for you

4. the flutter of fish and crabs in sun-pierced rockpools , the entanglement of ankles and feet in the sand, the striving desperation of touch

5. these, that I have made you; a mesh of wool and nylon and thread of glittering stars, the offering of hours of my hands, of warmth in winter, of skills I searched for only when alone, my fingers curled in softness

6. cocktails wrapped in little glass jars, delivered freshly to the doorstep, tied with instructions (we are all *Alice* here) the table set with greedy splashes of colour and beauty for no one but us

7. the tumble of keys under fingertips, community kept in my pocket, our living rooms a cinema with a crowd measured in households, synchronised movement, games plotted across states

8. pierogi, delivered fresh and steaming on the doorstep, the labour of φιλία, picture the quick fold of hands around dough, picture the care of preparation, picture the walk between houses with winter crisping your breath

9. the wilderness of the community garden, untended and tender, the hose a snake about my feet, hands twining the tomatoes into safety, the whispers of watching children floating through the glass

10. a countdown, *three, two, one* pretend my arms are looped around your neck, your face deep in the right angle between my shoulder and throat (can you feel me?), imagine we are in a garden, and the rain is soft and we are warm

Sumiko Saulson

BIO

Sumiko Saulson is an award-winning author of Afrosurrealist and multi-cultural sci-fi and horror. Ze is the editor of the anthologies and collections *Black Magic Women, Scry of Lust, Black Celebration*, and *Wickedly Abled*. Ze is the winner of the 2016 HWA StokerCon® Scholarship from Hell, 2017 BCC Voice Reframing the Other contest, and 2018 AWW Afrosurrealist Writer Award.

MOTIVATION

The birth of hir niece's daughter, Elune, hir brother's first grandchild, was hir inspiration.

WITH DECEMBER
COMES ELUNE

The dance of the Earth is eternal rebirth
From rot comes revival, for what it is worth
And the brilliant sun shines over all, over time
Over things we don't seek but enviably find

And this I find, true… life itself does renew
This is always the way, it erupts through decay
In the compost below, there are flowers that grow
In the garden of life, rife with perilous delights

For all of these reasons she is coming soon
The daughter of my brother's daughter; water breaking
Growth retaking barren land, of life partaking,
An oasis over desert sand that we may understand

What in March was conceived, small and yet unperceived
Will come to term in December, so when we remember
2020 in some distant future year, for our family
It will be the year Aluna finally appeared

Elune will be coming soon
Named for the African Goddess Moon
And though my niece lost a grandmother last year
My brother will be a grandfather once Elune is here

Angela Yuriko Smith

BIO

Angela Yuriko Smith is an American poet, publisher and author. Her first collection of poetry, *In Favor of Pain*, was nominated for an 2017 Elgin Award. Her novella, *Bitter Suites*, is a 2018 Bram Stoker Awards® Finalist. She co-publishes Space and Time magazine.

MOTIVATION

We were all caught up in this. None of us were alone. We just needed to be able to see each other.

A NEW MATCH

I stand at the edge
of the abyss—dark, cold, lost
with a single flame

to illuminate
the midnight chaos ahead.
Quivering candle

to drive away dark...
it will never be enough
to defeat the night.

I toss my pale light
into the pit where it falls
a wavering star

the ghost of a sun
plummeting past sad faces
I only now see.

Momentary shine
proves I am not all alone
on this precipice.

In absolute dark
a small spark makes a difference.
I strike a new match.

Ruby Smith

BIO

Ruby Smith is a Melbourne based poet and songwriter, currently finishing their Honours year in Philosophy at the University of Melbourne. Between writing, studying and composing, they spend their time cooking roast chickens at Woolworths, and convincing customers that masks are indeed mandatory.

MOTIVATION

To explore the unexpected loneliness of having to return to life post-isolation.

HOME ALONE

the first time I am alone in
        seven months
I lie on the floor of our cupboard
listen to the static in my ears

thank you for leaving me some cookies
you were right, I just ate one

I thought I liked being alone
but it turns out I am
        a stick figure traced
on the shower door

crushed, most gently crushed,
like cornflakes at the bottom of the box

I thought I liked being alone but
turns out I only like being alone
when being alone is with you

all poems are love poems
        now
I hope you're having a nice afternoon

Christina Sng

BIO

Christina Sng is a poet, writer, and artist. Her work has been widely published and exhibited around the world. She is the author of Bram Stoker Award® winner *A Collection of Nightmares, Astropoetry*, and *A Collection of Dreamscapes*. Christina lives in Singapore with her children and a menagerie of curious pets.

MOTIVATION

Even in our darkest moments, there is always light. There is always life.

OUR BRIEF TIME IN THE SUN

May the days
Be less weary for you
And the sunlight revive
But not burn you out

For our time in the sun
Is brief but sweet.
Each day,
No matter how hard,

I try to remind myself of that.

Heather Truett

BIO

Heather Truett is an MFA candidate and an autistic author. Her debut novel, *Kiss And Repeat*, releases in 2021. She has published poetry and short fiction with Tipton Poetry Journal, Panoply Zine, Drunk Monkeys, and others. Heather also serves on staff for The Pinch.

MOTIVATION

To capture the "peace of wild things" I find in this heron's presence.

GHAZAL FOR THE GOOD IN 2020

This year, I got to have breakfast with a great blue heron.
I realize I have lived a packed full life with too few herons.

Sipping coffee by the open window, this work from home world
is more than just precaution, more than the careful side I err on.

My friend turns in a poem for workshop, dreams that she is
a bird. A classmate tells her the poem is true, that's you, heron.

I want to be the peace of these feathers and beaks. I want
the pond in my yard to always be home base, from here on.

Everything has changed, but nature remains the same. She is not
a creature we can ever control. You cannot be subdued, my heron.

Heather, you may need to stand on one leg and wade in deep,
but you still can stand. There is beauty in the view of one blue heron.

Kyla Lee Ward

BIO

Kyla's poetry is collected in *The Land of Bad Dreams* and *The Macabre Modern*, from P'rea Press. Her work has been placed in the Australian Shadows and Rhysling awards. An actor and playwright, she has travelled widely and rhymed adventurously. Her interests include history, occultism and scaring innocent bystanders.

MOTIVATION

You can say what you want about the lockdown, but it was great for cleaning out cupboards.

WARDROBE MALFUNCTION

I have the dress. It is the perfect dress.
Now, I need somewhere to wear it.
An occasion worth shot taffeta
and a boned bodice.
My new shoes have scarcely left their box,
bought in anticipation of dinners and shows,
and maybe even the collapse of some great empire,
for which I must also wear my wings—in black, I think.
A bone mask
And finger blades, engraved.

Slightly less formal, but a lovely vintage piece,
this wrap will do for weddings, parties,
and accomplishing the death of gods.
It can be worn over shadows or a gilded rib-cage.
If I add fangs and maybe the heart of a star,
it's going to be a hot millennium!

I have outfits for every twist of fate—
a cincher for famine, hats for solar flares,
jackets for genocide and, come the next ice age,
a genuine fox fur stole. People can say what they wish.
What I don't have,
though my wardrobe has stygian depths,
Is something I can wear right
now.

Janeen Webb

BIO

Janeen Webb is a multiple award-winning author, editor, critic and academic who has written or edited a dozen books and more than a hundred essays and stories. She is internationally recognized for both her critical work and her fiction. She holds a PhD in Literature from the University of Newcastle.

MOTIVATION

We are living in a down-the-rabbit-hole scenario—I'm pretty sure there are metaphorical jabberwocks lurking in every quarantine hotel.

HOTEL QUARANTINA

Men without manicures designed
These hotel rooms. We cannot budge:
There's guards outside, but no clean air,
The food's not fresh - it's mostly sludge.

There's knuckle-nipping luggage racks,
A heel-trip in the entrance hall,
The power points are 'neath the desk,
Requiring tired guests to crawl.

The shower is high, above the bath,
With plumbing set to freeze, then scald,
And taps that simply won't oblige
Till Maintenance has twice been called.

The cistern buttons are a test,
Set flush against the bathroom tile,
The chrome so cleverly recessed
To snap a fingernail each time.

The towels are racked just out of reach,
The TV's showing ads, or porn,
The blackout curtains don't quite stretch,
Fast wi-fi is a hope forlorn.

Beware the lockdown traps, my dear,
The lamps that bite, the drawers that catch,
Beware the sticky carpet stains, and
Shun the mini-bar's deadly double latch.

Adam Wolfond

BIO

Adam Wolfond is a non-speaking autistic artist, prose-poet, featured on poets.org and exhibited in Toronto, Canada. He is the co-founder of dis-assembly in Toronto, a neurodiverse arts collective. His work can be viewed at esteerelation.com and also, dis-assembly.ca. His chapbook of poetry *In Way of Music Water Answers Toward Questions Other Than What Is Autism*, is available through his publisher, Unrestricted Editions.

MOTIVATION

Adam Wolfond spent time this year writing about the tumultuous events during the pandemic in 2020 and the paces needed to embrace diversity.

IN THE HEART OF MUSIC
OPENS HOPE

On thinking about the sickness I am easy
to think about healing and amazing hope.

I want to write that awesome hope lands
always calm thinking. Yes good wanting

of hope is the world really ready to day
the dance of love. I am thinking that I

answer the hope harnessing the way
labour of nurses always helps people.

The way inside is helping good
thoughtful healing and opens

the future for more singing and fun.
In song of the language I think in

melody and I pattern the language
to the leverage of thought that goes

into the heart of everything and I
to thank those who sing really wanting

song inside my rallying body.

Tabatha Wood

BIO

Tabatha Wood lives in Aotearoa, New Zealand. She writes weird, unsettling fiction and uplifting poetry, mostly under the influence of strong coffee.
A former English teacher and library manager, her first published books were written for professional educators. She now tutors from home while working as a freelance writer and editor.

MOTIVATION

Of Time and Tide was inspired by the proverb which states they wait for no man, and the feeling that while COVID made us feel like we had no control, we can all still strive to make good use of what time we have.

OF TIME AND TIDE

In the beginning, it felt like war.
As we sheltered in place inside our homes,
Fragile bubbles hunkered down, braced against the surge.
While the first waves rippled, seeking souls, as ravenous as wildfire.

We marked the days, we held the line. Five million soldiers strong.
Our kindness was our weapon — our courage and our strength.
But when every stranger on the street might pose a threat, concealed,
the sea became my solace. A saviour from the storm.

Feet that longed for freedom, walked, without a place in mind,
As I scaled the heights at my city's edge; lost in mist and gorse.
Beyond the harbour, mountain ranges spread their mighty weight.
Their peaks a jagged heartbeat of scratched lines across the skies.

The sea leans close to kiss the shore, embracing like old lovers,
and looking down on patchworked land—kaleidoscopes of green and blue—
From here, the ocean seems to breathe, inhaling as I do,
deep swallows of sharp, salted air. A prayer sent on the breeze.

When the time comes for me to leave, I want the tide to take me.
Scatter my ashes amongst the waves, I will follow where the ocean leads.
Until then, I will watch the horizon, becalmed with each new breath.
While dancing, ripples echo hope, as the surf rolls in to rest.

Fiona Wright

BIO

Fiona Wright's new essay collection is *The World Was Whole* (Giramondo, 2018). Her first book of essays *Small Acts of Disappearance* won the 2016 Kibble Award and the Queensland Literary Award for non-fiction, and her poetry collections are *Knuckled* and *Domestic Interior*.

MOTIVATION

Part of a months'-long conversation-in-poems exchange with poet Kate Middleton during the early pandemic, while we were both in precautionary quarantine and writing felt so useless and so hard.

& normal

new normal they say *new*
normal my housemate in the kitchen
in her headphones *new normal*
groans at the live-streamed pressers;
i keep hearing helicopters
and I can't tell if they're real.
each time i see a person
on the street i want to shake them;
each time i see a person
on the street i know that I am also
new normal a person on the street.
i have my first *new normal* dream
of isolation, where i'm constantly
reminded to stand distant
from my friends. we're in a queue
to see a play (dream logic loophole)
and my skin *new normal* hungers:
my throat feels dry and tired
hours after i close the screen. *new*
normal: i tell my doctors, this phrase
has rung, across my life –
new normal is old news   & normal
people are the ones who can't quite
fathom it, their uncontrol.

Marty Young

BIO

Marty Young is a Bram Stoker Award® nominated and Australian Shadows award-winning writer and editor. He was the founding president of the Australasian Horror Writers Association from 2005-2010, and one of the creative minds behind Midnight Echo magazine, for which he also served as executive editor until mid-2013. Marty's website is martyyoung.com.

MOTIVATION

For me to find a way through the horrors of 2020.

AN ENDLESS BARRAGE

News falls all around
Bombshells
Destroying our lives.
An endless barrage of
Chaos and doom and terror and—

I am exhausted.
Drawn out thin and transparent.
Eroding
And I cannot endure. I need to retreat
Back into my murder and mayhem.

But that world is closed to me,
(Or have I closed from it?)
At night, when my brain spoke loudest
all now I hear
Are screams.

I must stop reading, and yet start again.
Selecting nightmares.
Because that is how I will survive.
Let the world scream on
but I must stop screaming with it.

And let the mayhem find me

Only inside our creations
Where I can shelter from the carnage.
Finding my way whole
Through this endless barrage.